THE OLD
CONGREG

A Brief History of

THE OLD MEETING HOUSE

CONGREGATIONAL CHURCH

(founded in 1643)

≈~ Our Story So Far ~≈

John E. L. Clements

⌀

Parson's Porch Books

www.parsonsporchbooks.com

A brief history of the Old Meeting House Congregational Church (Founded 1643):
Our Story So Far
ISBN: Softcover 978-1-949888-21-8
Copyright © 2018 by John E. L. Clements

The Church was founded in 1643,
but the Chapel was not built until 1693
(after the 1689 Act of Toleration was passed).

The cover is a watercolour of the Old Meeting House Congregational Church, painted by Madeline Holt, a previous member of the Chapel. Her picture expresses the hope that you too will be able to meet God whilst walking up the long path to the Chapel – as the early Puritans did.

Hello, and welcome!

As the current Pastor of the Old Meeting House, I bid you warmly welcome to our ancient Chapel. It has been my privilege, over the years, to greet hundreds of visitors, and to paint word-pictures of our long history – which is not only enthralling, but also culturally significant. I myself am still learning about it. You, too, may have questions; and I believe the following pages will answer some of them.

Question One for most visitors is: "What's this *Book of Sports* I've heard about?" In this little guide, I will give a short explanation – as well as an overview of the Congregational Church, our beliefs, and significant aspects of our history. It will be a challenge with so few pages at my disposal; but I'm keen to spread the word about why this Chapel is such a cultural landmark – not only for Norwich and England, but for the Christian Church across the Atlantic.

I am not the first to point out that the word "history" is really "*His*-story". The Old Meeting House is a rich spiritual well, wherein many have imbibed the Waters of Life. As you spend time here on your visit, I pray that you may experience God's peace – and, at the same moment, receive a sprinkling of the faith of our Early Fathers, who lovingly built this Chapel during difficult days of our English Nation's history.

To find out more about the Independent (or Separatist) Church and its birthplace, Norwich, please visit www.oldmeetinghousechurch.org.uk

I remain,
Your Friend and Pastor,

John Clements

Contents

Let's have a quick walk around!

Our forecourt – formerly a burial ground – was made smaller when the Sunday School (now a private property) was built in 1842. It was reduced again around 1930, when the Peill Room was added.

On the right-hand side of the chapel we have the Golden Dog car park. Before 1962, that site was the vicarage garden of St Clements Church. Today, the former vicarage (in Colegate) houses the offices of Purcell's, an international company of architects.

In 1842, a century and a half after the erection of the Old Meeting House Chapel (referred to in this guide as "the Chapel"), the bicentenary of the founding of the Fellowship was celebrated. That same year, the Reverend Andrew Reed B.A. (Minister 1841–1855) laid the foundation stone of the two-tier School Hall situated to the south-west of the Chapel. Included in the celebrations was the sending of greetings – not only to the sister Church in Yarmouth, but also to a similar one in Rotterdam.

During the 19th century, there was, to the west of the Chapel, a day-school owned by the Fellowship of the Old Meeting House. Later controlled by the local Education Authority, the school has long since been demolished.

Now let's go into the Chapel. Its remarkable interior has changed very little over the years: a narrow vestibule stretches between the entrance doors, and there are access-ways to the galleries and ground floor. Beyond is the chapel: a simple auditorium, with pews, pillars, and pulpit of dark wood and walls of sober cream-coloured plaster. With an elegant staircase on each side, the pulpit occupies the centre, and looks down upon curving rows of pews, and up to galleries which encircle the three remaining walls standing upon Tuscan columns. Above them, other columns with Ionic capitals and quaint bits of entablature stretch to the ceiling.

Next to the western Gallery is an organ with gilt pipes and a handsome carved case. When I first came to the Chapel, the organ had been given a blue paint-job; but, thanks to the dedication of John Plunkett, who has spent at least 20 years restoring the organ, it has been (as he puts it) "resurrected". It was made by Robert Dallam around 1660, but did not arrive at the Old Meeting until 1838. I do hope you be will be able to hear it being played during your visit!

Preaching was, as we know, of great importance to the Puritans. Opposite the pulpit stands the South Gallery, with its large octagonal clock. Was it placed there, I wonder, to ensure that preachers kept an eye on the time? – Sermons were often long; and the pews were never comfortable!

On the other side of the pulpit, two black grave-slabs have been mounted upon the wall: one (from an earlier church building) to the memory of John Coney, and the other to John Lucas. They died in 1658 and 1703 respectively. By contrast, the tablet over the pulpit, with its white sarcophagus on a black oval, shines out like a little jewel – a monument to the Reverẽd Samuel Newton (d. 1810), carved by a little-known Norwich sculptor, Joshua Cushing. On the same wall are two by John Ivory, commemorating the Reverend Thomas Scott (d. 1746) and John Dawson (d. 1721).

Other memorials are under and above the galleries: to Jeremiah Tomson (d. 1721), described as "a great admirer of Free Grace"; to Thomas Theobald, maker of dyes, "one of the principal manufacturers"; and to John Jarrold (d. 1852), who had been a deacon at the Chapel, and also founded the Jarrold Printing Company.

What is a Meeting House?

The Puritans wanted to distinguish between "a church" – a body of people who believe in and follow Jesus Christ – and "a meeting house or chapel", which is a building where "the church" meets.

Meeting Houses were very plain, with no statues or pictures of the Saints (as could be seen in many medieval Anglican and Roman Catholic places of worship). The Puritans' purpose was to keep the attention focused inwards – on the spiritual nature of worship – rather than outwards on the building.

What's so special about Norwich?

In the 16th and 17th centuries, Norwich was considered to be the second most important city in England after London. Around 1580, Robert Harrison was the Master of the Great Hospital (founded in 1249). His contemporary and friend Robert Browne also resided there, and started one of the first Separatist churches. His followers were known as Brownists. At their height, they numbered about 20,000. Memorably, Shakespeare referred to them in his play *Twelfth Night*.

Browne wrote two notable works. First: *A Treatise of Reformation without Tarying for Anie* (approximate translation: "What do we want? Reformation! When do we want it? Now!"). Second: *A Booke which Sheweth the Life and Manners of All True Christians.*

In the *Treatise*, he asserted the right of the Church (i.e. the believers themselves) to effect necessary reforms without authorization of any civil magistrate. In the *Life and Manners*, he set out the theory of "Congregational Independency". Both were published at Middelburg in 1582; and both played an important role in establishing the model for the Christian Church in America.

In August 1603, John Robinson became the associate Pastor of St. Andrew's Church in the commercial centre of Norwich. Some months later, he was ejected from the Church, and gathered together a group of people whom became known as The Pilgrim Fathers.

Fleeing religious persecution in England, they spent several years in Holland. In 1620, many of that group sailed to America in the *Mayflower* – and the teachings of John Robinson went with them, playing a historic role in the New World's new churches.

Robinson himself ultimately died in England, because his escape ship, the *Speedwell*, proved unseaworthy. In any event, he was one of the early leaders of the English Separatists, and is thus also regarded as one of the founders of the Congregational Church.

During the English Civil War (1642 – 1648), East Anglia was a stronghold for Cromwell's "New Model Army" – most of whose soldiers were Puritans. The Old Meeting House was among the most influential churches in England at the time, with a membership of around 350.

───── ✦ ─────

Who were the Puritans?

The Puritans were a widespread and diverse group who took a stand for religious purity in the 16th, 17th, and 18th centuries across Europe and America. Their rise was directly related to the increased knowledge that came to the general population in the Age of Enlightenment. As people learned to read and write, so the Bible became more accessible to commoners, and many began to read for themselves (a habit that was strongly discouraged in the established church). Some Puritans had links with Anabaptist groups in continental Europe, but the majority were connected with the Church of England.

The word Puritan was coined in the 1560s as a derisive term for those who advocated more purity in worship and doctrine. In England, Puritans believed that the English Reformation had not gone far enough and that the Church of England was still tolerating too many practices associated with the Church of Rome (such as hierarchical leadership, clerical vestments, and the arcane rituals of the state church). Many Puritans advocated separation from all other Christian groups, but most were "non-separating" and desired to bring cleansing and change to the church from within.

Holding a high view of Scripture, and deeming it as the only true law of God, Puritans believed that each individual, as well as each congregation, was directly responsible to God, rather than answering through a mediator such as a priest or bishop. The Congregational Church in America is a direct descendant of the early Puritan settlers, and any modern group that advocates Congregational rule and individual piety has been influenced in some way by Puritan teaching. Even today, theologians from many church backgrounds appreciate reading the works of the old Puritan divines, even if they differ in some points of doctrine.

Both America and Great Britain owe a debt to the Puritans for the foundations they laid that gave us the framework for our Christian freedom of worship today. Philosophies such as the "divine right" of kings gave way to individual liberties and the recognition of the rights of the common man. The "Yankee work ethic" came about because of the belief that a man's work is done first for God's approval. The belief in public education comes from the Puritans, who founded the first school in America (Roxbury, 1635), as well as the first college (Harvard, 1639), so that the common people would be able to read the Bible for themselves. The moral foundations of the early United States came from the emphasis by Puritan leaders on godly behaviour.

William Bridge M.A. (1600 – 1671)

His name is strongly associated with the Old Meeting House, and he is known to have drawn up the Covenant in 1643. (Though he had spiritual oversight of the fellowship, there is no evidence that he was ever the minister.) After Bishop Wren, an Anglican, ejected Bridge as rector of St. Peter's Tombland in Norwich, he spent some time in Rotterdam. Returning to England in 1642, he accepted a position as town preacher in Yarmouth, where he organised an Independent Church, and formally became its Pastor. In 1662, however, he was again ejected from the pulpit – this time by the Act of Uniformity.

Independents who lived in Norwich chose to walk to Yarmouth (20 miles away) to attend meetings, but in 1643 were able, under Bridge's leadership, to form a group here at the Old Meeting House in Norwich.

Bridge was an excellent preacher and an able scholar. We know that he rose at 4 a.m. every day to search the Scriptures, confess his sins, and pray to God. He often studied for 17 hours a day, yet is remembered as being one of the greatest pastoral Puritans. He also wrote more than 36 books: the best known, *Lifting Up Of the Downcast*, has sold over 6 million copies, and remains in print to this day!

Bridge was often called to preach before the Long Parliament (1640 – 1660), and was consulted by it on Church-related issues. He also served on the same committee as John Owen, Chaplain to Cromwell's New Model Army.

St Peter's Hungate and St George's Tombland

Bridge spent his last years at Yarmouth and in Clapham, Surrey, where he preached for an Independent Church, which he probably founded. Reportedly, people flooded to hear him in such numbers that, by 7 a.m., no more could be packed in! He died, in Clapham, on 12th March 1671.

What was the Covenant of 1643?

On June 28th of 1643, William Bridge and the co-founders of the church entered into the following covenant – the foundation of the Old Meeting Fellowship:

"We, being desirous in the fear of God, to worship and serve Him according to His revealed will, do freely, solemnly, and jointly covenant with the Lord, in the presence of His saints and angels.

"That we will forever acknowledge and avouch God for our God in Jesus Christ.

"That we will always endeavour through the Grace of God assisting us, to walk in all His ways and ordinances, according to His written Word, which is the only sufficient rule of good life for every man, neither will we suffer ourselves to be polluted in any sinful ways, either public or private, but abstain from the very appearance of evil, giving no offence to the Jew or Gentile, or Churches of Christ.

"That we will all love, improve our communion as brethren, by watching over one another, and as need be, counsel, admonish, reprove, comfort, relieve, assist, and bear with one another, humbly submitting ourselves to the government of Christ in His churches.

"Lastly, we do not promise these things in our own, but in Christ's strength; neither do we confine ourselves to the words of this Covenant, but shall at all times account it our duty to embrace any further light on truth, which shall be revealed to us out of God's Word."

Statement of Faith

(as printed in the Trust Deeds of the Old Meeting House)

1. The divine inspiration of the Holy Scriptures and their sole authority and entire sufficiency as the rule of faith and practice.

2. The unity of God with the proper deity of the Father, Son, and Holy Ghost.

3. The universal and total depravity of man in the sight of God and his exposure to eternal death as the wages of sin.

4. The incarnation of the Son of God, the sufficiency of His atonement for sin and free justification by faith alone in Him.

5. The absolute necessity of the Holy Spirit's grace and power for man's regeneration and sanctification.

6. The predestination according to God's gracious purposes of a multitude that no man can number unto eternal salvation which in no way interferes with the use of means or man's responsibility.

7. The immutable authority of the law of God as the rule of human conduct.

8. The immortality of the soul, the resurrection of the dead and the final judgment when the wicked shall go away into everlasting punishment, but the righteous into life eternal.

What was the Book of Sports?

Nearly every visitor to the Old Meeting House Chapel asks this question after reading the plaque on the wall behind the pulpit: "Rev. William Bridge...left the Church of England rather than read the Book of Sports (1637)."

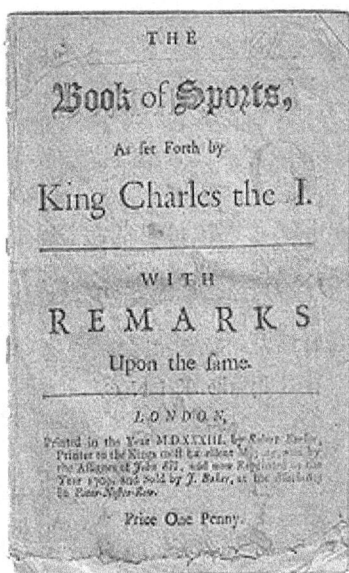

The Book of Sports, or *Declaration of Sports*, was issued in 1617 by King James I (in collaboration with Thomas Morton, Bishop of Chester). It listed sports and recreations permitted on Sundays and other "holy days", with a view to bringing about a peaceable solution to arguments between the Puritans and "the gentry" (mainly Catholics) in Lancashire. This initially local law was extended to the whole of Britain in 1618. All clergy were obliged, every Sunday morning, to read the book to their respective congregations, who were then encouraged to pursue such activities as archery and dancing. Also considered harmless on the Sabbath were: May-games, Morris dancing, the setting up of May Poles, and the drinking of ales. For women, decorating a church with rushes was added to the list.

James' son, King Charles I, re-issued the Declaration in 1633, under the cumbersome title: *The King's Majesty's Declaration to His Subjects Concerning Lawful Sports to be Used*. Some commentators suspect that the reissued version was penned by the newly-installed Archbishop of Canterbury, William Laud; but he denied it. Indeed, the main text differs little from the original issued by James; so it could be described as a mere "make-over".

Bishop Wren (a relative of Sir Christopher Wren, architect of St Paul's Cathedral in London) presided over the Norwich Diocese between 1635 and 1638. He hated the Puritans, and severely enforced the legal duty to read and implement the Book of Sports. For ministers who refused to do so, the penalty was removal from office. But, during the lead-up to the English Civil War, anger against the Declaration grew at the same rate as Puritan power; and, with the fall of Laud in 1640, its legal force was abolished. Three years later, it was publicly burned. Two years after that, Laud was executed.

❦

A (partial) List of the Chapel's Ministers

Surprisingly, we know more about the Founders and early Pastors than we do about the later Ministers (i.e. from 1768 onwards). Research to complete the records is ongoing. This guide may be updated in due course!

Timothy Armitage was called to the Pastorship on 26th July 1647. He had been a lecturer at St. Michael's Church, Coslany (currently a disused church at the other end of Colegate). Under his tenure at the Old Meeting House, the membership rose to around 350. He also published *Tryall of Faith of the Woman of Canaan*; and *Enock's Walk with God*. He died in December 1655. One year afterwards, a volume containing nine of his sermons was published by his successor, Thomas Allen, entitled *The Son of God walking in the fire with the Servants of God.*

Thomas Allen M.A. became the minister in 1656 and continued until his death in 1673. He was the author of *The Way of the Spirit in Bringing Souls to Christ.*

Robert Asty was Pastor in 1673. He published *The Ordinary Matter of Prayer, Drawn Into Questions and Answers*; and two treatises: first, *Of Rejoicing in the Lord Jesus in all Cases and Conditions*; and second, *Of a Christian's Hope in Heaven, and Freedom from Condemnation by Christ.*

John Cromwell held office between 1675 and 1685. He is thought to have been a cousin of Oliver Cromwell. Beyond that, little is known of his ministry.

Rev Martin Fynch was Pastor from 1685 to 1697. After the 1689 Toleration Act, he played a key role in the building of the Chapel that we now call The Old Meeting House – among the first such Chapels in the country. (To the right of the pulpit, you can see a plaque dedicated to him.) He wrote numerous books, including *A Manual of Practical Divinity* (1658); *A Treatise of the Conversion of Sinners* (1680); *An Answer to Mr. Thomas Grantham's [...] Dialogue between the Baptist and the Presbyterian* (1691); and *A Funeral Sermon for [...] John Collinges, D.D.* (1695). The facts of his life, so far as they are known, are recorded on his tombstone:

"Here lieth waiting for the resurrection of the just,
The body of the late Reverend
MR. MARTIN FYNCH,
who was a burning and a shining light,
a plain and spiritual
and powerful preacher of God's word.
He walking humbly and closely with his God,
Full of goodness and love,
Courteous and pitiful to all men,
Beloved and reverenced by all;
He, having feared the Lord from his youth,
and laboured abundantly,
In the ministry of the gospel 49 years,
and guided this church of Christ 12 years
with great wisdom and integrity,
diligence and faithfulness,
and many years desired to depart hence,
and to be with Christ;
Being worn out with the pains of the stone
His soul ascended to keep an everlasting Sabbath,
on the 13th February 1697,
in the 70th year of his age.
If we believe that Jesus died and rose again, even
so them also which sleep in Jesus
will God bring with him.
1 Thess. iv. 14"

John Stackhouse became co-Pastor with Mr. Fynch in 1690 and remained until 1709. His tombstone informs us that he laboured in the ministry for thirty-nine years – seventeen of them as Pastor at the Old Meeting House.

Thomas Scott presided from 1709 to 1746, and is buried in the Chapel, at the foot of the pulpit stairs. Dr Doddridge (see below) says of him: "The death of Mr. Scott, of Norwich, touched me very nearly; I believe he was one of the holiest and most benevolent men upon the earth."

Abraham Tozer held office from 1747 to 1754, and was a student of Dr Doddridge. At this time, Puritans were not permitted to study at Oxford or Cambridge; thus they set up their own Academies. One of the best known was that run by Dr Philip Doddridge in Northampton.

Samuel Wood D.D. ministered from 1754 to 1767, and was also a student of Dr Doddridge.

Samuel Newton 1768 – 1810

William Hull 1809 - 1823

Stephen Morell 1824

John B Innes 1825 – 1837

J.H. Godwin 1837 – 1839

Andrew Reed B.A. 1841 – ~~1837~~ 1855

John Hallett 1856 – 1878
Robert Hobson 1878 – 1891

John Lewis 1892 – 1903

J.J. Brooker 1904 – 1926

R.E.F. Peill M.A. was Pastor from 1929 – 1930, and had previously been a missionary attached to the China Inland Mission. He died in the Chapel whilst preaching a sermon. The Peill room was built in his memory.

S. John Bates 1930 – 1936

P.J. Lawton B.A. 1937 – 1945

E.T.D. James M.A. 1946 – 1952

S.D. Gamson 1954 – 1962

G.A. Johnson 1964 – 1969

Jack Burton ministered from 1970 – 1975. Author of *Transport of Delight*, he was also a regular contributor to the religious column of the local *Eastern Daily Press*.

Roy C.P. Hunt 1979 – 1986

E. Ritchie 1992 – 1994

John Clements Th.D 1995 – 1997

Frank Little 2000 – 2015

John Clements Th.D 2015 – and still Pastoring!

Under the Curtain of Oppression

We witness a shadow-land, with figures in twos and threes picking their way through orchards and gardens and narrow streets. A door opens and closes intermittently, without noise and without light. More figures have entered the house than it can comfortably accommodate. Newcomers flit to neighbouring houses, in which the dividing walls have been drilled with holes so that the occupants can hear one another. A moment of quietness: and then one voice is raised alone; raised in prayer, reading, and preaching. There is no singing: street spies are lurking with ears cupped, tuning in for such sounds.

Stationed at external corners, friends are on watch, alert to give warning to the worshippers. At a later hour, the preacher is silently conveyed away; and the congregants disperse into the shadows as quietly as had come – but with a glow in their hearts.

Thus was the nature of daily existence for the fathers of those who built the Old Meeting House: manoeuvring to found their Church in days when the law forbade them to erect a building, and subjecting them to all manner of penalties for the mere fact of being Nonconformists and Dissenters. And thus do we acquire a sense of the resolve and enthusiasm that has enabled this Church to survive three-and-a-half centuries – with many more to come as it fulfils its historic mission.

The Pilgrim Fathers and Norwich

The group that we now call the Pilgrim Fathers (the name was not coined until decades afterwards) were a group of about sixty Nonconformists who sailed to America on the Mayflower in 1620.

For centuries, there had been Christians who believed that the Church was moving away from its New Testament roots. They had come to consider it a power structure, existing by dint of pomp and elaborate liturgy, and imposing its will upon the common people. Folks who made their own decisions regarding religion were called heretics (a Greek-rooted word meaning "chooser"). The Reformation ushered in certain changes in the teaching about Salvation; but the Reformed Churches themselves were now starting to impose doctrines and practices – as had Roman Catholicism before them.

St. Andrew's was one of Norwich's most prominent churches. In 1603, John Robinson (1575-1625) became a member of its clergy; but, within a year, he was forced to leave Norwich. He led a Separatist church in the Trent Valley until 1609, when he was again forced to flee, this time taking his congregation to Leiden in Holland, where they were free to worship according to their conscience. And yet, notwithstanding the Netherlands' reputation of offering freedom to all, problems eventually arose – whereupon Robinson's followers resolved to emigrate to the New World.

The Virginia Company held the right to authorise settlements along the coast as far north as latitude forty-one. Robinson sent two men to London in order to negotiate with the Virginia Company, to ask King James to grant them a charter for a new colony, and to raise a company of shareholders to back their venture.

Only fifty of Robinson's church opted to make the first crossing. He himself decided to stay with the remainder, and make the crossing later. On 31 July 1620, they sailed from Delftshaven on the *Speedwell*. At Southampton, they joined the *Mayflower*, which was carrying a further twenty Separatists and about fifty other passengers. However, the *Speedwell* was found to be unseaworthy, and had to return for repairs: first to Dartmouth and then to Plymouth. In the end, most of the pilgrims abandoned the *Speedwell* and crowded onto the *Mayflower*. A few could not be accommodated, and had to stay behind. That group included John Robinson.

On 16 September 1620, the *Mayflower* finally set sail from Plymouth in the English Channel. Because of a navigation error, they arrived, on 16 November, at Plymouth Bay on the coastline of the New World – far north of latitude forty-one. The Pilgrims considered this a happy co-incidence: the name "Plymouth" had been bestowed by John Smith a few years earlier; and they decided to retain it.

The Separatists and other emigrants stayed together...but tensions were to arise. Five of the

25

original party had died on the journey; forty-five others perished during the first six months. Over the next few years, more settlers from Leiden arrived – among them, one of Robinson's sons. (As mentioned earlier, Robinson himself died in England in 1625. His church there eventually dispersed, integrating with the Dutch community.)

The *Mayflower* returned to England in 1621, and was scrapped a couple of years later. Many buildings in England are said to incorporate timber from her; but there is no evidence to support these claims.

Pilgrim Fathers (and Mothers) from East Anglia

Desire Minter had gone to Leiden and worked for the Carver family. At the time of the New World crossing, she was aged about twenty (the average age on board being thirty-two). She returned to England (perhaps to Norwich; we're not sure) in 1625. **William Holbeck** was employed in some capacity by **William White**, and went to the New World with him (whether from Leiden or Norwich is not known). **Edward** and **Ann Fuller** originated from Redenhall in Norfolk, and became members of the Leiden Church. Their son, **Samuel**, was born in Leiden. **Thomas Williams** hailed from Great Yarmouth, went to Leiden, then to the New World. **Edward** and **Elizabeth Winslow** were from Chattisham in Suffolk and sailed directly from there.

Democracy: Planted by the Pilgrim Fathers?

Emphatically not! The Congregational or Separatist Churches were not democratic, and never claimed to be. They believed that, having been chosen by God, they were obliged to preserve a particular way of life at all costs. Anyone who didn't fit in to the New World settlement was driven out of it.

If the honour of establishing New World democracy should go to any single individual, Roger Williams is probably the man. Williams is rarely mentioned in Church history books, but a short biographical note and extracts from his writings can be found in the more comprehensive anthologies of American literature.

The churches formed by the Pilgrim Fathers were usually governed by the members of the congregation, and hence became known as Congregational churches. (There were many on both sides of the Atlantic.) In 1972, an Act of Parliament allowed the majority of the approximately 4,000 Congregational churches to merge with Presbyterian churches and become the United Reformed Church (URC); but around 900 chose not to. Among those was Norwich's oldest Chapel, the Old Meeting House in Colegate, which endures as a separate congregation. Very many American visitors who tour Europe on the "Pilgrim Trail" tend to consider the Old Meeting, rather than St. Andrew's, as their own closest link to Norwich.

The part played by the eastern counties of England in the Pilgrim movement may need some elucidation. In the 17th Century, they were (with the benefit of hindsight) the most progressive counties of England. The Eastern Association, of which Cromwell became joint-Commander, included Norfolk, Suffolk, Essex, Hertfordshire, Cambridge and Huntingdonshire. It was from these counties that Cromwell drew his Ironsides, "captains...who knew what they fought for and loved what they knew." The proportion of the Mayflower Pilgrims originating from those counties is striking: 6 came from Yorkshire, 9 from Nottinghamshire, 2 from Lincolnshire, 17 from London, 17 from Kent, 11 from Essex, and 32 from Norfolk.

<hr />

The Founding of Saybrook in 1673

The following (slightly adapted) extract is from the book History of Congregationalism and Memorials of the Churches in Norfolk and Suffolk *(1877), by John Browne. In that book, Browne quotes Hallet's* History of the Old Meeting House *(date unknown):*

At the time of the death of Thomas Allen, a most interesting event happened in connection to the Chapel. A band of emigrants from Norwich and the neighbourhood emigrated to America, most of whom were members from the Old Meeting, and formed a settlement in the neighbourhood of the Mohegan Indians, which was Saybrook, from the names of Lord Say and Lord Brook, leaders of the colony. These settlers came to a peaceful and honourable arrangement with the aboriginal tribes, purchased the requisite territory from them, and at a later period had secured to them and their descendants a considerable tract of land. Our pious ancestors had not long dwelt in Saybrook before they began to instruct the Indian tribes in the doctrines of Christianity, who received the Gospel from them, and still inhabit the territory assigned them, having a neat place of worship, and regular dispensation of the means of grace.

Beyond these tribes was another race, called the Naragansett Indians, who were often at war with the Mohegans. The latter were frequently obliged to call in the help of their white allies. On one occasion, when hard pressed by their foes, a summons was sent to Saybrook, and thirty men were despatched, under a Mr. Seffingwell, in a canoe by night. About 14 miles up the river, they encountered and vanquished the Naragansett warriors. The Mohegans, out of gratitude to their deliverers, voluntarily gave them, after this action, an allotment of ground 10 miles square, at the junction of the two branches of the river, now called Thames, at the mouth of which is New London. A town soon arose on the territory given by the Mohegans, which the settlers called Norwich, in the records of which may still be seen the original deed of gift, signed by the Mohegan chief Uncs, with his royal mark, the tortoise.

It is impossible to estimate the sufferings to which these godly men and women were exposed for righteousness' sake, first the bitter persecution which, raging more and more fierce, at length forced them to leave their native country and all they deemed dear; next, in the perils of a voyage, when navigation was less familiar – the vessels they procured being inferior in accommodation to the best which the age could furnish; then in the disembarkation on the shores overgrown with thick forests down to the very beach, in the face of subtle and cruel hordes of savage Indians, and of every description of venomous and horrid animals; and then in the rough labours of clearing and cultivating the ground, and hewing out the first steps to the platform of civilization. But the God they worshipped smiled upon them, and now "the little one has become a thousand."

<hr />

What is a Congregational Church? How does it differ from the Church of England?

Visitors to our shores may be puzzled by the differences between the many different Christian denominations.

At www.oldmeetinghousechurch.org.uk, you'll find articles which go into greater detail than we have space for here; but I will attempt a brief overview.

Before the reign of King Henry VIII (1491 – 1547), England had been a Roman Catholic country. Henry was born and brought up a faithful Catholic; and, in 1521, Pope Leo conferred on him the title *Fidei Defensor* (Defender of the Faith) – the title still held by our current monarch, Queen Elizabeth II.

It was Henry's failed marriage to Catherine of Aragon that drove him to break away from the Roman Catholic Church and to declare himself, in 1534, the

Supreme Head of the Church of England (which is the offical state church to this day).

During Henry's time, the Bible was being translated into English; and people like William Tyndale (1494 – 1536) were openly challenging the traditional teachings of the Roman Church. During the reign of Elizabeth I (Henry's daughter),* the Protestant movement, which had started in Europe, rose to dominance in England. It was against this backdrop that, in 1580, the Norwich resident Robert Browne (see **What's so special about Norwich?**, above) was able to start his group known as the Brownists.

How does all this relate to our Chapel? Well, Congregationalism is a form of Protestant Christianity which asserts the principle that a local congregation is completely autonomous under God, and should not, therefore, submit to external authorities such as Bishops (which Church of England congregations do). We also maintain the practice of infant baptism (which Baptists do not). Perhaps most significantly, there is no ecclesiastical hierarchy.

In 1718, local Congregational churches in England and Wales numbered a mere 229. By 1851, they had increased to 3,244. Moreover, Congregational and Baptist growth was clearly surpassing the growth of the population. They went from 2.28% in 1718 to 7.70% in 1851. No surprise, then, that some of the Victorian era's most respected Evangelical ministers (such as **J.A. James**) and some of its most popular preachers (such as **Thomas Binney**) were Congregationalists. **R.W. Dale**, one of the finest Victorian theologians outside the Church of England, was also a Congregationalist.

* – 1558 –1603 .

Knowing all this, you might now be asking: What makes a Congregationalist? Well, I don't think there's any particular mindset. **John Milton** and **Robert Browning** were poets. **Oliver Cromwell** was a Parliamentarian, soldier and mystic. **Daniel Defoe** (educated at a Dissenting Academy) was one the first novelists – as was **John Bunyan**. **Isaac Watts**, whose hymns we still love to sing here at the Old Meeting, was one of the first popular hymn-writers. There have also been philantropic industrialists like **Lord Leverhulme** (of Port Sunlight fame) and **Sir Titus Salt** (of Saltaire); **Benjamin Waugh,** founder of the NSPCC; penal reformers like **John Howard**; explorers such as **David Livingstone**;missionaries like **Gladys Aylward** (portrayed in the film *Inn of the Sixth Happiness*); and the athlete **Eric Liddell** (of *Chariots of Fire* fame). What they hold in common, if anything, is a freedom from conventionality underpinned by an independence of mind – a quality seeded in them, we might speculate, by Congregationalism.

To complete this brief overview: the Anglian Church is based geographically on the parish system, and liturgically on Creeds; whereas the Congregational Church is a gathered, non-creedal church.

Here at the Old Meeting, our 1643 Covenant is seminal. We commemorate God's Covenant with us, and ours with Him; but we also bear in mind our earthly covenant to each other, as members of the church.

The Old Meeting House today

As you walk into this simple but historic Chapel, you may notice a poster which memorably declares: *"This chapel is not a museum for saints but a hospital for sick souls."*

We hold a number of regular meetings. For **worship,** the Chapel opens every Sunday at 3pm. On the third Tuesday of the month, we have **hymn-singing** at the Doughty's Hospital, situated next to the Chapel (and, remarkably, built 3 years before it). On the third Saturday of the month we have **Sing on Saturday** at 3pm, when, to the accompaniment of the wonderful old organ, we sing traditional hymns – and then have fellowship over tea and coffee. On the second Monday of every *alternate* month, at 7pm, we have **Light From Old Times** – a series of talks from guest speakers on aspects of history and the Puritan faith. This too is followed by fellowship over tea and coffee. (All the talks are now recorded, and you can hear them by visiting our website.) Additionally, we hold concerts at which you can hear the mellow tones of our wonderful 17th Century organ throbbing through the Chapel's galleries!

The future is built on the past

The times of tribulation for the Old Meeting may be long gone; but we believe the golden times are just around the corner! Recent years have seen an international revival of interest in the Puritans. In

Norwich, we are in the process of forming a charity, "The Old Meeting House Foundation", which will, we hope, raise the global profile of the Chapel, and thereby extend its ministry to satisfy the growing interest.

A final word

I want to thank you for taking the time to read this short Introduction to the Old Meeting House Congregational Church in Norwich, England. Sadly, we live in an age when most people know very little about the history of their church; nor do they realise the many benefits they can gain by studying it.

Many of the Old Testament writers use a technique that we may call "Recounting the acts of God". (One example, if you would like to read it, is the entirety – seventy-two verses! – of Psalm 78.)

Our God is the God of our history: that which He has done in the past, He can do again in the future. The Old Meeting House was built by men and women who knew first-hand what spiritual persecution felt like; yet they retained their overwhelming faith in an all-powerful God. Furthermore, they were led by spiritual giants (see **A (partial) List of the Chapel's Ministers** above). Many of our Church's members not only shaped the spiritual life of England, but also contributed to the religious foundations of America.

As a Pastor, I have found that those who don't follow spiritual giants can end up as spiritual pigmies! If you know anyone who wishes to avoid such a fate, perhaps you could advise them to purchase of copy of William Bridge's 1648 tome **Lifting Up for The Downcast** (now published by Banner of Truth Books). Its thirteen chapters are a commentary on a single verse of Scripture: Psalm 42 verse 11, "Why are you cast down, O my soul, and why are you disquieted within me? Hope in God; for I shall again praise him, my help and my God."

For my part, I pray that this booklet, short though it is, may have given you an insight into your spiritual heritage...and thereby kindled a yearning to learn more about the riches to be explored in the Old Meeting House, the City of Norwich, the county of Norfolk, the Islands of Britain, and the multiple groupings of the Congregational Church at home and abroad.

I hope you will visit our website (constantly updated): www.oldmeetinghousechurch.org.uk.

Perhaps the website will inspire you to visit this historic Chapel in person. We would love it, too, if you would like to keep in touch by email and ask for details of how to become a Friend of the Old Meeting House. info@oldmeetinghousechurch.org.uk,

Now let's read more about the Puritans

Here are a few good books to start with:-

> *The Puritans: Their Origins and Successors* – D.M. Lloyd-Jones. The Banner of Truth (first published 1987, reprinted 1991).

> *The Genius of Puritanism* – Peter Lewis. Soli Deo Gloria Publications (first published 1977, reprinted 1996).

> *The Mayflower Pilgrims: Roots of Puritan, Presbyterian, Congregational, and Baptist Heritage* – David Beale. Ambassador-Emerald International (2000).

> *Meet the Puritans: With a Guide to Modern Reprints* – Joel R. Beeke & Randall J. Pederson. Reformation Heritage Books (first published 2006, reprinted 2007).

> *A Puritan Theology: Doctrine for Life* – Joel R. Beeke & Mark Jones. Reformation Heritage Books (2012).

THIS CHAPEL IS NOT A MUSEUM FOR SAINTS * BUT A HOSPITAL for SICK SOULS

The Old Meeting House Prayer

The Old Meeting House Congregational Church stands today not only as a fine specimen of the architectural taste of the 17th century, but also as a worthy memorial to our fathers in the Faith. Let us who come within its walls spare time to offer this brief prayer.

"Almighty and Everlasting God, we thank You for this House of God and Home of men. Grant it increasing usefulness in the service of Your Kingdom. We thank You, too, for those who, in times of darkness, kept the lamp of faith burning; for great souls who saw visions of larger truth and dared to declare it; for all who fought for truth and liberty; for the quiet and gracious souls who were a blessing to many; for preachers raised up to declare the message of God with power; and for all faithful witnesses to the life that is in Christ.

O God, to us may grace be given
To follow in their train;
through Jesus Christ our Lord."

Amen.

Additional Quotes

The Reverend Andrew Reed B.A, who was minister at Old Meeting House from 1841 – ~~1837~~ 1855 likened the Old Meeting House to the brook Cherith mentioned in 1 Kings chapter 17, "whose waters shall not be dried up, but with purer, stronger, wider, and more fertilizing current shall form one of those millennial streams wherewith the whole earth shall be watered as a fruitful garden of the Lord."

"In the time of His presence we have the sense of His love to us. But in the time of His absence then He sees, and we ourselves have the sense of, our love to Him."

The following quotes are from William Bridge, founder of the chapel.

"A praying man can never be very miserable, whatever his condition be, for he has the ear of God; the Spirit within to incite, a Friend in heaven to present, and God Himself to receive his desires as a Father. It is a mercy to pray, even though I never receive the mercy prayed for."

"I will tell you what small, weak, little grace will do, and not do, to distinguish it from common grace. It will not oppose much grace; the least spark of fire will not oppose the flame or resist the flame. Water will, because fire and water are contrary: and so, false grace will oppose the highest degree of grace, saying, why need you be so strict and precise? You may go to heaven with less ado: but the least degree of true grace will not oppose the highest. True grace loves examination. It loves to examine, and to be examined; for it is sincere, and sincerity is much in examination."

"If I work in my calling for mine own profit only, then I walk with myself therein; but if I do all for God's glory, not mine own profit, then I walk with God in my calling."

"Of all books, study the Bible;
of all duties, be much in prayer;
of all graces, exercise faith;
of all days, observe the Lord's day;
and of all things in heaven and earth,
be sure that you get an interest in God by Jesus Christ."

The hedges of the State or Church are the laws... Those enemies of yours or ours, that have or would tread down our hedges even to the ground, shall not ever go unpunished. When the hedge is lowest the serpent is nearest."

"every man, who loves the truth, should bear his testimony for it."

"Happy is the man whose gifts do cherish his graces, and whose graces do produce gifts: and as diversities of gifts should not make us disagree or envy one another, but rather bind us in in love to one another."

CPSIA information can be obtained
at www.ICGtesting.com
Printed in the USA
LVHW020751131219
640345LV00007B/89/P

9 781949 888218